Feng Shui Fundamentals

Health

Lillian Too

ELEMENT

Shaftesbury, Dorset • Rockport, Massachusetts • Melbourne, Victoria

First published in Great Britain by
ELEMENT BOOKS LIMITED
Shaftesbury, Dorset SP7 8BP

Published in the USA in 1997 by
ELEMENT BOOKS INC.
PO Box 830, Rockport, MA 01966

Published in Australia in 1997 by
ELEMENT BOOKS LIMITED
and distributed by Penguin Australia Ltd
487 Maroondah Highway, Ringwood, Victoria 3134

Designed and created with
THE BRIDGEWATER BOOK COMPANY LIMITED

ELEMENT BOOKS LIMITED
Editorial Director Julia McCutchen
Managing Editor Caro Ness
Production Director Roger Lane
Production Sarah Golden

THE BRIDGEWATER BOOK COMPANY LIMITED
Art Director Terry Jeavons
Designer James Lawrence
Managing Editor Anne Townley
Project Editor Andrew Kirk
Editor Linda Doeser
Picture Research Julia Hanson
Studio Photography Guy Ryecart
Illustrations Isabel Rayner, Andrew Kulman, Mark Jamieson, Michaela Blunden, Paul Collicutt, Olivia Rayner, Jackie Harland

Printed and bound in Hong Kong

British Library Cataloguing in Publication Data available

Library of Congress Cataloging in Publication data available

ISBN 1 86204 117 2

The publishers wish to thank the following for the use of pictures:
Dean Conger/Corbis, p 19; Elizabeth Whiting Associates, p 31; Julia Hanson, p 49; Image Bank, pp 15, 51; and Zefa, pp 6, 7, 9, 15, 34/5, 46,7, 48/50.

Special thanks go to:
Bright Ideas, Lewes, East Sussex
for help with properties

Lillian Too's website addresses are
http://www.asiaconnect.com.my/lillian-too
http://www.dragonmagic.com

Lillian Too's email addresses are
ltoo@dragonmagic.com
ltoo@popmail.asiaconnect.com.my

CONTENTS

WHAT IS FENG SHUI?

AN INTRODUCTION TO FENG SHUI FOR HEALTH

風水

Feng shui is the practice of creating harmony in your living environment to bring about happiness, success, and good health. It is based on abstract Chinese concepts of humankind's relationship with the universe. This requires the integration of cosmological thought with the philosophies expounded in ancient texts, such as the I Ching, and the interpretation of important ancient symbols, such as the eight-sided Pa Kua and the nine-sector Lo Shu grid. Feng shui seeks to create environments with an abundance of the life force, known to expert practitioners as sheng chi or in more colorful language the dragon's cosmic breath.

When sheng chi flows smoothly in and out of all living and non-living things within a household, productive and happy events are the result. Occupants will benefit from the dragon's benevolent breath; good luck comes into the home, incomes are enhanced, and careers proceed smoothly. Relationships will bring happiness and the personal well-being of people living within the home is safeguarded. All of this results from the constant flow of good energy that embraces the home.

Blockage of the sheng chi produces the opposite result. Still worse, being hit by shar chi, the killing breath will bring grave misfortune. This is manifested in the occupants of the home suffering from severe and constant ill-health, as well as quarrelsome relationships and financial loss. Life thus becomes unbalanced and unhappy.

When sheng chi flows smoothly, the mind and body are filled with energy and all relationships will be in harmony.

THE CONCEPT OF CHI

The abstract concept of chi penetrates all branches of Chinese traditional practice. Chi has no form, no shape, and is invisible, yet through it, all things on earth that affect people's well-being manifest themselves. Physical decay is the gradual disintegration of chi and death is the total absence of it.

Traditional Chinese practices, whether feng shui, acupuncture, or chi kung, all focus on protecting and nourishing chi, both externally and internally. Chi kung teaches that nourishing chi within through internal exercises effectively supplements health and longevity. Similarly the protection of chi inside the home will lead to harmony, prosperity, and longevity.

These ideas are based on the belief that all things in the universe, both alive and inanimate, possess chi. Every room, every house, every building – all natural and manmade spaces – are believed to contain energy that has its own unique form of chi. In external environments, the quality of chi is affected by the nature of the land - mountains, hills, and rivers – while inside the home, the quality of chi varies depending on its orientation, the items present in each room, as well as how they are arranged in relation to each other. Thus analyzing the landscape becomes important in assessing external feng shui and scrutinizing the orientation of the home and the arrangement of furniture becomes highly significant in interior feng shui.

The placement of entrances, exits, doors, and windows all affect the quality of the chi: whether it is vibrant, fresh, and alive with energy or stale and fatigued, hostile or damaging. Doors, especially main doors, become particularly crucial in the practice of feng shui.

The corners and center of any room have subtle variations in the type of chi present. This reflects the influence of the five elements, a theory of Chinese abstract thought. All things on earth are categorized into five elements, from compass directions and locations to different internal organs of the body, from seasons to mountain ranges. Thus, there will be fire chi, water chi, earth chi, metal chi, and wood chi. These types of chi affect different aspects of the human condition and their subtle activation represents one of the most interesting dimensions of feng shui practice.

THE CHINESE PERSPECTIVE OF HEALTH AND LONGEVITY

Longevity and a life of good health have preoccupied the Chinese since time immemorial. Chinese traditional practice is replete with doctrines and techniques that address this aspect of human life. There are numerous legends and folk stories describing the search for immortality. Ancient rulers were reported to have sent emissaries throughout the kingdom in search of the elixir that would bring them eternal life. Legend has it that the emperor Huang Ti sent three thousand virgin boys and girls on a ship sailing into the eastern seas to look for the islands where the peach of immortality grew. Needless to say, those young emissaries were never heard of again and some believe they subsequently became the ancestors of the present-day Japanese. There are also many popular legends associated with the adventures of the Eight Immortals, characters regarded as saints and who feature strongly in Chinese homes either in pictures or in china or metal ornaments to symbolize long life for the residents.

The Chinese pantheon contains many gods of longevity.

Through the centuries, however, the search for immortality gave way to more realistic goals and, eventually, techniques that could be practiced to lengthen the life span of people were developed. These techniques drew on the Chinese abstraction of chi. The old sages pronounced that not only was chi present in the natural environment, it was also the force that defined life itself, so that the physical body was said to be alive because of the presence of chi. In addition, when total harmony exists between the environmental and human chi, a long, happy life would result.

LONGEVITY

Feng shui is concerned with engendering an atmosphere conducive to achieving good health, which always implies living to a ripe old age. Longevity was regarded as a very important component of good fortune. To be able to reap the harvest of a lifetime's work, to remain alive to see sons and daughters married and gain recognition, to enjoy the pleasures of grandchildren, and to see the family line continue are some manifestations of this kind of good fortune. Consequently, emblems of longevity abound in the Chinese gallery of symbols and gods of longevity feature prominently in the Chinese pantheon.

It follows that if the human chi was strong and balanced, the health of the physical body would be excellent, but if the chi was blocked, it would cause sickness. When chi was extinguished altogether, it resulted in death.

This approach toward the health of the body resulted in the development of various sets of movements that exercised both the muscles and the five vital internal organs of the body. The organs were likened to the five elements: the heart was of the fire element, the lungs were metal, the kidneys were water, the liver was wood, and the spleen was earth. There are exercises, such as chi kung, tai chi chuan, and Taoist revitalization methods, which concentrate on creating a harmonious balance of energies in these organs. These exercises are practiced to this day.

Many different meditation techniques were also developed that focused on improving circulation and clearing blockages, both mental and physical, that caused illness. Like the blockage of chi within the living space causing harm, so too, it was believed, that if the body's circulation is obstructed, the harmonious flow of chi within it would be severely affected, causing aches and ailments to develop.

The Chinese also developed breathing methods that focused on attracting further vital energy into the body through points along its meridians, a network of channels carrying chi through the body. Energy breathing was seen as a vital component of the healing process and it was considerably enhanced when there was also a harmonious link with the energy that permeated the environment.

Tai chi chuan is one of the exercises used to maintain and regulate the flow of chi.

Yang energy represents the outer regions of the body and heat. Yin energy represents the internal organs of the body and cold. Both yin and yang each contain a kernel of the other.

YIN AND YANG ENERGIES IN ILLNESS

Classical textbooks on Chinese traditional and herbal medicines usually describe disease and illness in terms of yin and yang. Disease is diagnosed as being caused by an excess of either yin or yang energy.

Too much yin or yang in the atmosphere or the foods we eat results in antagonistic energies attacking the body. These hostile energies in the environment are described as atmospheric. When they are in opposition to the energy of the human body, there will be a conflict between the two opposing sets of energies and illness is often the result of this struggle. For residents of any space to enjoy good health, the energies of that space must harmonize with those of the physical bodies occupying it.

"Wind" is described as a hostile yang energy. It is regarded as the major cause of many different types of illnesses, including the common cold. The Chinese often diagnose a variety of ailments as being caused by wind and, therefore, treat these ailments by rubbing what is termed "wind oil" (an example is tiger balm oil) around the upper orifices of the body (nose and navel).

"Wind water" is a more severe form of hostile yang energy. This is when wind has not been properly treated and has succeeded in penetrating the body. It is a dangerous situation because the hostile yang energy will, by then, have reached the inner regions of the body – the internal organs that represent the yin energy of the body. The symptoms reflect this affliction and the illnesses that result will require expert treatment with herbal or other medicines and the services of a sin seh or doctor.

Yin and yang energies must be kept in balance to maintain a healthy environment.

Hostile yang energy may result from an excess of yang energies, either within the body through the intake of too much yang (heating) food, or in the environment because of unbalanced feng shui. It is most common during the hot summer months, when a combination of heat and dampness often causes havoc to the vital balance of yin and yang in the atmosphere.

Harmful yin energy occurs during the winter months. Cold is most harmful to yang energy, which circulates in the superficial regions of the body. Thus, when yin cold attacks the body, the first part hit is the yang energy. If the yin energy defeats the yang energy, the pores of the body become blocked and body heat cannot escape, thereby accumulating within the body.

The Chinese diagnosis of illness and disease also distinguishes between yin summer heat and yang summer heat, and between yin winter cold and yang winter cold. The differences are subtle and to understand properly these nuances of diagnosis requires close analysis of the principles of Chinese medicine. For our purposes, it is sufficient to note that a balance of yin and yang must be maintained if we wish to create an atmosphere that is so full of healthy energy that sickness will find it difficult to take hold.

Chinese herbal medicines are used to treat hostile yang energy.

FENG SHUI FOR HEALTH

USING THE PA KUA

八卦

Activating the luck of longevity and good physical health starts with understanding the Pa Kua symbol, which is the most important tool of feng shui practice.

In the Early Heaven arrangement, the Pa Kua is believed to be a powerful protective tool and merely hanging it above the main door outside the home is deemed sufficient to deflect any hostile energies that may be threatening the home and its residents.

However, the Pa Kua is also a reference tool for analysis. This eight-sided emblem corresponds to the four cardinal points of the compass and the four subdirections. In addition, each side has

THE TREE OF LIFE

Reminiscent of other cultures, the Tree of Life is often depicted on carpets. This would be a suitable object to place in the east to symbolize the trigram Chen.

concentric rings of symbols that bring great meaning to the Pa Kua, including a specific trigram. Trigrams are symbols made up of three parallel lines; these lines may be solid yang or broken yin lines. Their relationship to each other gives meaning to the trigrams. The Pa Kua in the Later Heaven arrangement is used to analyze living space and correct an imbalance of yin and yang

THE DIRECTION EAST

Chen is the growth trigram that represents good health. According to the Later Heaven Arrangement, it is placed in the east. This is the corner of any home or room that represents good health for the family. If this corner has good feng shui, family members, especially the breadwinner, will enjoy excellent health and will live to a ripe old age. If this corner has bad feng shui, however, all kinds of illnesses will befall family members, who literally take turns at becoming ill or going in and out of hospital. The family breadwinner will also lack longevity luck, unless the astrological readings are very strongly indicative of a long life.

Feng shui for good health thus starts with an examination of the east sector of the room or home and, in particular, the meaning of the trigram Chen.

CHEN

This trigram represents the eldest son. It has two yin lines above a single unbroken yang line. Chen also signifies spring, which is a season of growth. In the language of the ancient Chinese text, the I Ching, Chen stands for the "arousing", characterized by great claps of thunder bursting in the spring sky, waking creatures from hibernation, and causing the life-giving rains to fall. Chen is a happy trigram that also suggests laughter and happiness. It has great strength and energy.

That it stands for growth and vigor is what makes it representative of life itself. Activating the corner that houses this trigram attracts healthy growth energies. The direction is east and the element is big wood, suggestive of trees rather than bushes, a deep green color rather than light green, and large wooden structures (furniture) rather than small wooden objects (ornaments).

PRODUCTIVE CYCLE

The illustration here shows the productive cycle of the five elements - earth, metal, water, wood, and fire. Water, the element that produces wood, is in a positive position in relation to the wood element and is therefore helping to energize wood, which is associated with health and family relationships.

APPLYING FIVE ELEMENT ANALYSIS

The best method of energizing the east, and so energizing the luck of good health, is to apply the rationale of the five elements. According to the classical texts, all things in the universe, tangible or intangible, belong to one of five elements. These are fire, wood, water, metal, and earth. They are said to interact with each other in never-ending productive and destructive cycles. Applying element analysis to feng shui requires an understanding of how the cycles work and how they may be applied practically.

THE WOOD ELEMENT

The element of the east corner is wood, symbolized mainly by plants. Identifying the relevant element to activate is a vital part of the application. It suggests that placing a healthy plant in the east will activate excellent health luck for residents of the home. Moreover, from the cycles shown here, you will see several other attributes of the wood element.

- Wood is produced by water, so water is said to be good for it.
- Wood itself produces fire, so fire will exhaust it.
- Wood is destroyed by metal, so metal will be harmful to it.
- Wood destroys earth, so earth is overcome by it.

DESTRUCTIVE CYCLE

The illustration here shows the destructive cycle of the five elements. Wood is being overwhelmed by metal, the element that destroys wood. This means that wood, which is associated with health and family relationships, is not being strengthened.

From these attributes we know that to strengthen the element of the east, we can use all objects that symbolize both wood and water, but should strenuously avoid anything belonging to the metal element. Delving deeper, we see that the east is represented by big wood. This suggests that the intangible forces of the wood in this corner are strong, powerful, and not easily overcome. Big wood is suggestive of very strong growth.

Wood is the only one of the five elements that is alive and capable of reproducing itself. This implies that the yang energies of its corner, although not immediately evident, are nevertheless strong. This is eloquently suggested by the lines of the trigram where the unbroken yang line lies hidden under two yin lines. Using inanimate objects made of wood can thus be as effective as using plants for energizing this corner.

THE GREEN DRAGON

Because the east is also the abode of the green dragon, placing a decorative dragon carved out of wood, or made of china, would be an auspicious feng shui feature in this corner.

ENERGIZING THE WOOD ELEMENT

Each of the five elements is activated by the presence of objects belonging to the same group. Plants, especially healthy-growing plants that look green, lush, and well cared for, are probably the best symbols to use to stimulate the wood element of the east health corner.

If you are fortunate enough to have land around your home, try growing a clump of bamboo in the east corner of your garden. Bamboo is one of the most popular Chinese symbols of longevity and strength. Any variety is fine, but keep the bamboo well cultivated from season to season.

Plant a window box of flowering plants if there is a window in the east corner of the room you wish to activate. This will attract healthy yang energy into the room.

These should ideally be living plants, although realistic-looking silk or other artificial plants are also quite effective. It is important to avoid using dried plants or artificial plants that look dead or have gathered so much dust that they suggest a sad stagnation of energies. Artificial plants that depict a plant in winter are also ineffective. The idea is to symbolize healthily growing plants – the way they look in spring.

You can also place a small plant on a table top in the east corner if the room is small. In feng shui always be aware of the need for balance. Activating any element should not be overdone. Thus plants placed in a room should never seem to overwhelm it.

If there is an edge in the east part of the room being activated, caused by a protruding corner, a square pillar, or a piece of furniture, place a plant, such as the one shown here, against it. This not only serves to deflect the harmful energies created by the sharp edge, but also simultaneously stimulates the vibrancy of the wood element. Over time, the plant may lose its vigor and even wilt and die. If so, throw it out and place a fresh, new plant there.

DISPLAYING SYMBOLS OF LONGEVITY

Among the pantheon of Chinese deities, Sau, the God of Longevity, is perhaps one of the most popular. He is one of the three star gods often used together in Chinese homes. These deities are rarely actually worshipped. Their presence in a Chinese home is to create the energies associated with their symbolic presence. Sau himself is also often displayed on his own, not necessarily in the east corner of the room, although this would be a good idea. Sau can also be placed facing the main door to attract healthy long-life vibrations into the home.

The God of Longevity is depicted as a smiling old man with a broad forehead. He carries a staff and is often shown with a deer (another symbol of longevity) and some peaches (the fruit of longevity). It is extremely easy to find a figurine of Sau in the Chinese supermarkets of many Western cities and if you are visiting China, Hong Kong, or Taiwan, do use the opportunity to acquire a statue of this deity. He brings enormous good luck and the statues are carved in ivory or wood, cast in bronze, or made from cloisonné or ceramics. Sau is also painted on ceramic jars and is a popular subject of Chinese painting. Indeed, it is considered extremely appropriate to present the God of Longevity as a gift to celebrate the birthday of the bread-winner. Such a gift implies a wish for long life.

Sau, the God of longevity, can be found diplayed in many Chinese homes. The Chinese believe his presence will help them to enjoy a long and healthy life.

The deer is another symbol of longevity. It is often depicted with the Chinese God Sau.

THE PEACH, THE DEER, AND THE CRANE

The peach features prominently in all the Chinese stories and legends of immortality. It is believed that the peach tree that bears the fruit of immortality lies in the garden of the Queen of the West, Hsi Wang Mu. The Eight Immortals are believed to have stolen into the garden and tasted it.

The peach tree is also regarded as being an auspicious plant and is often featured in paintings and objects d'art. It is a good idea to display ornamental peach bushes made of inexpensive jade, which are readily available from Chinese supermarkets.

The deer is almost always featured with the God of Longevity, although beautiful wood carvings of deer are also available. The symbolism of the deer originates from its close association with Sau.

The cranes of longevity have red foreheads. They are almost always depicted as a flock, either flying or standing in water with one leg tucked under them. Cranes are also often drawn with the pine tree, yet another symbol of long life. If you can obtain a painting of these beautiful birds, hang it in the east corner.

Images of cranes, such as this sculpture in Beijing, symbolize longevity.

THE CELESTIAL ANIMALS HEALTH EXERCISES

天獸

Orientating your home according to the principles of feng shui can be effectively supplemented with the simple health exercises developed by the Shaolin and Tai Chi Masters. The movements of these exercises were designed to allow the human body to create the vital breath, termed chi. Many of these are very simple exercises and they are named after the celestial animals, the dragon, tiger, phoenix, and turtle, and for the longevity creatures, the deer and crane. The Turtle Exercise falls into both categories and is featured on page 25.

Anyone can use these exercises to maintain balanced physical and emotional states. However, if there is a specific problem affecting an internal organ, select the appropriate exercise according to the five elements theory to bring healing energies to the afflicted organ concerned. The heart is of the fire element, the lungs metal, the liver wood, and the spleen and stomach are of the earth element.

This exercise addresses the fire element and is excellent for creating healing energies in the spleen, stomach, and all the muscles of the body. These represent the earth element. The exercise also helps overcome feelings of anger, anxiety, and hostility, and strengthens the heart. The method is free-form and relaxed. Hold the pose as long as you can and repeat several times.

The recommended time is half an hour each morning. You will feel your palms

---

This is the second stage of the dragon exercise. It is also excellent for firing your ambitions and motivating you, but in a very relaxed, non-stressful way. The method is very simple and involves cycles of breathing. Do nine cycles.

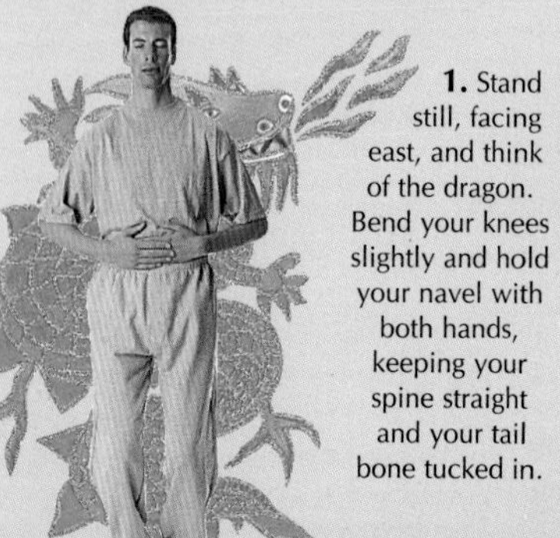

1. Stand still, facing east, and think of the dragon. Bend your knees slightly and hold your navel with both hands, keeping your spine straight and your tail bone tucked in.

THE RELAXED DRAGON EXERCISE

1. Stand still with feet as far apart as your shoulders. Take a few deep breaths and visualize yourself as a dragon.

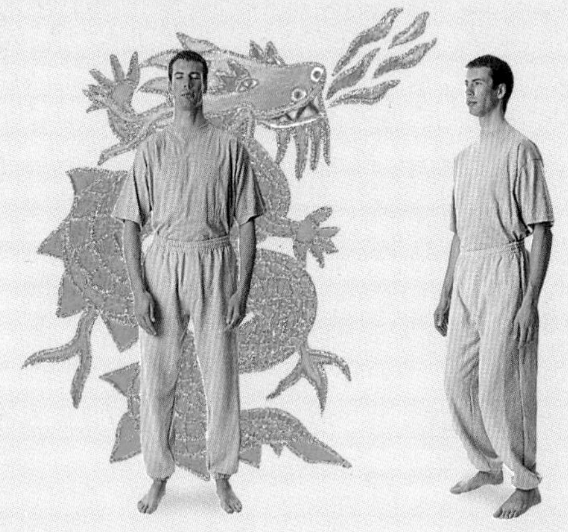

2. Bend your knees very slightly, keep your spine straight and pull your tail bone in. Let your arms hang loosely by your sides, with palms facing inward. Breathe normally, let the mouth relax and keep the tongue gently touching the top of the palate. Stand like this for as long as you can.

tingle slightly and, after about ten minutes, you will feel the chi moving up your hands. With time and practice the chi will move down into the tan tien, in the navel area, where it is believed all human chi is stored. This exercise is the first stage exercise of many different types of Chinese martial arts.

THE BREATHING DRAGON EXERCISE

2. With your left hand on your stomach and the right palm covering the left hand, breathe in through your nose and feel the breath going into the stomach. Do this very slowly!

3. Feel the stomach expand like a drum or a balloon.

4. When you cannot breathe in any longer, bend forward 15–25 degrees and breathe out slowly at the same speed that you inhaled. Breath out until your stomach feels hollow. Straighten. This is one cycle of breath.

THE FLYING PHOENIX EXERCISE

This exercise is associated with the metal element and is useful in overcoming melancholia and depression, which, if not addressed, could lead to lung problems. The phoenix is said to have the ability to rise from the ashes and soar effortlessly to great heights. This exercise cheers the soul considerably – be aware of the chi moving as you do it. This is a wonderful exercise and you will feel your palms tingle within a few minutes. This is the chi slowly gathering energy in your palms before moving inward and filling you with a sense of well-being. The recommended time for holding this pose is about 15 minutes each morning.

1. Stand still, keeping the spine straight, the tailbone tucked in, with your feet apart and the knees slightly bent. Imagine yourself as a phoenix.

2. Extend your arms horizontally outward, as if spreading your wings ready to fly.

3. Keeping your arms flexed, gently raise your hands to form a right-angle. Keep your palms facing outward, absorbing the chi of the surroundings. Let your tongue rest gently at the top of your mouth and hold this pose for as long as you can.

THE CRANE

The red-combed crane is a popular symbol of longevity and the ancients believe it was the bird's unique pose – standing on one leg, with the other folded into its belly – that gave it the ability to survive on all kinds of diets. They were convinced that the pose stimulated its stomach and internal organs, thereby strengthening the digestive, respiratory, and circulatory systems. So, the exercise, involves standing on one leg.

THE HAPPY PHOENIX EXERCISE

This is also referred to as the one-hundred year movement or pak sau kung. This exercise is believed to be so good for heath, those who do it faithfully each morning will live to be 100 years old! It is very simple exercise and takes only ten minutes to do.

1. Stand straight with your left leg half a pace in front of the right. and your feet apart the same width as your shoulders.

2. With the knees slightly bent, the spine straight, and the tail bone tucked in, extend both arms straight in front, palms down.

3. Bend forward and down slowly to about 20 degrees, with the spine still straight (not curved). At the same time, allow your arms to swing back rather like preparing to dive into a pool. Look down as you bend forward.

4. Straighten. Do this movement nine times.

EXERCISE

1. Stand with the feet together with toes and heels touching. Place the sole of one foot on the calf of the other leg.

2. Slowly work the foot up to the inner thigh. Then slowly raise both hands above your head, inhaling as you do so. Join your hands and hold this position as long as you can.

THE MAGICAL TURTLE

The turtle is one of the four celestial animals in feng shui cosmology. Together with the green dragon, the white tiger, and the crimson phoenix, the black turtle is part of the important quartet that symbolically defines excellent landscape feng shui. Like the other creatures, the turtle is an important feng shui tool.

The turtle is also very important for its role in bringing the Lo Shu square to the world. An old Chinese legend describes how the numbers of the square were brought to humankind on the back of a turtle that emerged from the River Lo many thousands of years ago. The Lo Shu square is the tool that unlocked the secrets of the Pa Kua symbol.

The turtle symbolizes several wonderful aspects of good fortune that make life pleasant, but its most outstanding attribute is as a symbol of longevity. There is a wonderful legend about the turtle that describes how, with a minimum of movement, it conserves its energy, reduces its need for sustenance, and lives to a thousand years old.

The turtle also symbolizes support. Its direction is actually the north and the element associated with it is water. This makes its presence in the east sector, the corner that represents good health, extremely compatible. Place a model of a turtle in the east if you want to benefit from the wonderful good-health energies that its presence brings to the home.

TURTLES AND TURTLE SUBSTITUTES

Turtles are frequently used to activate good feng shui. If turtles are not easy to come by, it is just as acceptable to put a tank of terrapins in the east corner. Remember that feng shui places great emphasis on symbolism, so even a painting or a print of a turtle would be effective.

THE TURTLE EXERCISE

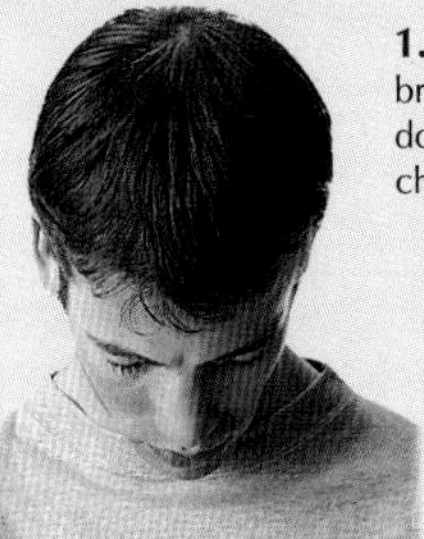

1. Relax and then bring your chin down on to your chest.

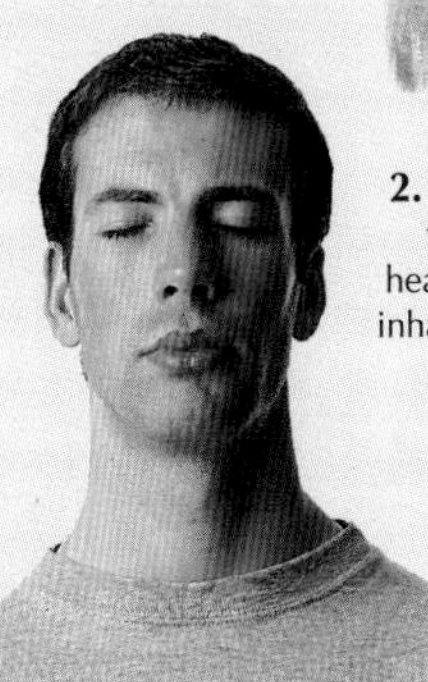

2. Stretch the top of your head upward, inhaling at the same time.

3. Bring your head further back, while simultaneously exhaling.

Repeat eight times.

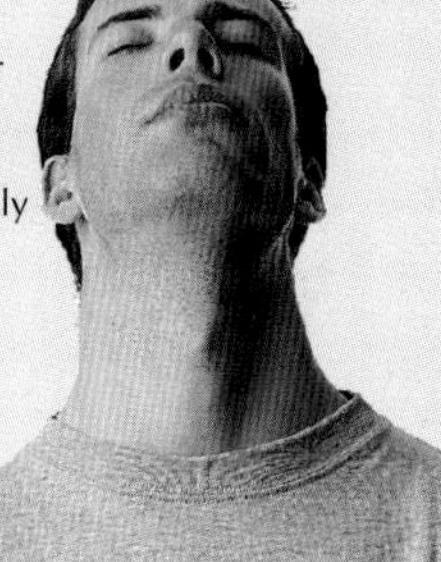

Legend tells of a turtle that lived deep in a cave with a family who had been trapped there during a landslide. The family, it is said, survived for 800 years by emulating the turtle's minimal movements. Indeed, they discovered that virtually the only movement the turtle made was to extend and retract its head in and out of its shell. Occasionally, it would extend its tongue to catch a drop of water from the ceiling of the cave. By copying the turtle, the family survived through the centuries, their story spread, and soon became a legend.

From the story came the Turtle Exercise, which is incorporated in many Chinese health systems. It may be done sitting or standing.

INDIVIDUAL HEALTH DIRECTIONS

THE COMPASS FORMULA

指南針

Your heavenly health direction, based on your date of birth, can be calculated using a powerful compass feng shui formula. It is derived from the two ancient symbols of feng shui – the eight-sided Pa Kua, with its layers of meanings, and the Lo Shu magic square, a nine-sector grid that further unlocks the secrets of the Pa Kua. It is also known as the Pa Kua Lo Shu formula (Kua formula for short).

The exact method of activating the personal health luck directions was a closely guarded secret for many years. This method was given to the author's feng shui Master by an old Taiwan Grand Master, who was a legend in his time. According to the feng shui Masters, everyone's personal health direction and location can be activated to achieve excellent health luck. This means sleeping and sitting in a direction that allows the person to capture his or her tien yi, which is literally translated as "the doctor from heaven direction." Capturing this implies enjoying a state of physical and mental fitness. This formula is ideal for people who are constantly tired and lethargic, and also helps alleviate those suffering from illness, although the focus of feng shui practice is on prevention rather than cure.

If your Kua number is:	
1	east group
2	west group
3	east group
4	east group
5	west group
6	west group
7	west group
8	west group
9	east group

THE KUA FORMULA

To determine your health direction, first determine your Kua number. Obtain your Chinese year of birth based on the calendar on pages 28-29, and use this calculation to get your Kua number. Remember that there is no Kua number 5 in this system, although it is included here for clarity. Males with Kua number 5 should use number 2, and females should use number 8.

Your health orientation is:

North for both males and females

Southwest for both males and females

East for both males and females

Southeast for both males and females

Southwest for males and
Northeast for females

Northwest for both males and females

West for both males and females

Northeast for both males and females

South for both males and females

THE KUA FORMULA

Add the last two digits of your Chinese year of birth. e.g. **1956, 5+6=11**.
If the sum is higher than ten, reduce to a single digit; thus **1+1=2**.

Males	**Females**
Subtract from	Add
10	**5**
thus	thus
10-2	**5+2**
=8	**=7**
So, for men born in	So, for women born in
1956	**1956**
the Kua number is	the Kua number is
8	**7**

Now check against this table for your family direction and location.

THE CHINESE CALENDAR.

Note that the Chinese New Year begins in either late January or early February. When calculating your Kua number, do take note of this. So if you were born in January 1946 before the New Year, your Chinese year of birth is 1945, not 1946. This calendar also indicates the ruling element of your year of birth. This gives you further clues on which corner of the home, based on your element, will have the most effect on your well-being.

Year	From	To	Element	Year	From	To	Element
1900	31 Jan 1900	18 Feb 1901	**Metal**	**1923**	16 Feb 1923	4 Feb 1924	**Water**
1901	19 Feb 1901	17 Feb 1902	**Metal**	**1924**	5 Feb 1924	24 Jan 1925	**Wood**
1902	18 Feb 1902	28 Jan 1903	**Water**	**1925**	25 Jan 1925	12 Feb 1926	**Wood**
1903	29 Jan 1903	15 Jan 1904	**Water**	**1926**	13 Feb 1926	1 Feb 1927	**Fire**
1904	16 Feb 1904	3 Feb 1905	**Wood**	**1927**	2 Feb 1927	22 Jan 1928	**Fire**
1905	4 Feb 1905	24 Jan1906	**Wood**	**1928**	23 Jan 1928	9 Feb 1929	**Earth**
1906	25 Jan 1906	12 Feb 1907	**Fire**	**1929**	10 Feb 1929	29 Jan 1930	**Earth**
1907	13 Feb 1907	1 Feb 1908	**Fire**	**1930**	30 Jan 1930	16 Feb 1931	**Metal**
1908	2 Feb 1908	21 Jan 1909	**Earth**	**1931**	17 Feb 1931	15 Feb 1932	**Metal**
1909	22 Jan 1909	9 Feb 1910	**Earth**	**1932**	16 Feb 1932	25 Jan 1933	**Water**
1910	10 Feb 1910	29 Jan 1911	**Metal**	**1933**	26 Jan 1933	13 Feb 1934	**Water**
1911	30 Jan 1911	17 Feb 1912	**Metal**	**1934**	14 Feb 1934	3 Feb 1935	**Wood**
1912	18 Feb 1912	25 Feb 1913	**Water**	**1935**	4 Feb 1935	23 Jan 1936	**Wood**
1913	26 Feb 1913	25 Jan 1914	**Water**	**1936**	24 Jan 1936	10 Feb 1937	**Fire**
1914	26 Jan 1914	13 Feb 1915	**Wood**	**1937**	11 Feb 1937	30 Jan 1938	**Fire**
1915	14 Feb 1915	2 Feb 1916	**Wood**	**1938**	31 Jan 1938	18 Feb 1939	**Earth**
1916	3 Feb 1916	22 Jan 1917	**Fire**	**1939**	19 Feb 1939	7 Feb 1940	**Earth**
1917	23 Jan 1917	10 Feb 1918	**Fire**	**1940**	8 Feb 1940	26 Jan 1941	**Metal**
1918	11 Feb 1918	31 Jan 1919	**Earth**	**1941**	27 Jan 1941	14 Feb 1942	**Metal**
1919	1 Feb 1919	19 Feb 1920	**Earth**	**1942**	15 Feb 1942	24 Feb 1943	**Water**
1920	20 Feb 1920	7 Feb 1921	**Metal**	**1943**	25 Feb 1943	24 Jan 1944	**Water**
1921	8 Feb 1921	27 Jan 1922	**Metal**	**1944**	25 Jan 1944	12 Feb 1945	**Wood**
1922	28 Jan 1922	15 Feb 1923	**Water**	**1945**	13 Feb 1945	1 Feb 1946	**Wood**

Year	From	To	Element
1946	2 Feb 1946	21 Jan 1947	Fire
1947	22 Jan 1947	9 Feb 1948	Fire
1948	10 Feb 1948	28 Jan 1949	Earth
1949	29 Jan 1949	16 Feb 1950	Earth
1950	17 Feb 1950	5 Feb 1951	Metal
1951	6 Feb 1951	26 Jan 1952	Metal
1952	27 Jan 1952	13 Feb 1953	Water
1953	14 Feb 1953	2 Feb 1954	Water
1954	3 Feb 1954	23 Jan 1955	Wood
1955	24 Jan 1955	11 Feb 1956	Wood
1956	12 Feb 1956	30 Jan 1957	Fire
1957	31 Jan 1957	17 Feb 1958	Fire
1958	18 Feb 1958	7 Feb 1959	Earth
1959	8 Feb 1959	27 Jan 1960	Earth
1960	28 Jan 1960	14 Feb 1961	Metal
1961	15 Feb 1961	4 Feb 1962	Metal
1962	5 Feb 1962	24 Jan 1963	Water
1963	25 Jan 1963	12 Feb 1964	Water
1964	13 Feb 1964	1 Feb 1965	Wood
1965	2 Feb 1965	20 Jan 1966	Wood
1966	21 Jan 1966	8 Feb 1967	Fire
1967	9 Feb 1967	29 Jan 1968	Fire
1968	30 Jan 1968	16 Feb 1969	Earth
1969	17 Feb 1969	5 Feb 1970	Earth
1970	6 Feb 1970	26 Jan 1971	Metal
1971	27 Jan 1971	15 Feb 1972	Metal
1972	16 Feb 1972	22 Feb 1973	Water
1973	23 Feb 1973	22 Jan 1974	Water
1974	23 Jan 1974	10 Feb 1975	Wood
1975	11 Feb 1975	30 Jan 1976	Wood
1976	31 Jan 1976	17 Feb 1977	Fire

Year	From	To	Element
1977	18 Feb 1977	6 Feb 1978	Fire
1978	7 Feb 1978	27 Jan 1979	Earth
1979	28 Jan 1979	15 Feb 1980	Earth
1980	16 Feb 1980	4 Feb 1981	Metal
1981	5 Feb 1981	24 Jan 1982	Metal
1982	25 Jan 1982	12 Feb 1983	Water
1983	13 Feb 1983	1 Feb 1984	Water
1984	2 Feb 1984	19 Feb 1985	Wood
1985	20 Feb 1985	8 Feb 1986	Wood
1986	9 Feb 1986	28 Jan 1987	Fire
1987	29 Jan 1987	16 Feb 1988	Fire
1988	17 Feb 1988	5 Feb 1989	Earth
1989	6 Feb 1989	26 Jan 1990	Earth
1990	27 Jan 1990	14 Feb 1991	Metal
1991	15 Feb 1991	3 Feb 1992	Metal
1992	4 Feb 1992	22 Jan 1993	Water
1993	23 Jan 1993	9 Feb 1994	Water
1994	10 Feb 1994	30 Jan 1995	Wood
1995	31 Jan 1995	18 Feb 1996	Wood
1996	19 Feb 1996	7 Feb 1997	Fire
1997	8 Feb 1997	27 Jan 1998	Fire
1998	28 Jan 1998	15 Feb 1999	Earth
1999	16 Feb 1999	4 Feb 2000	Earth
2000	5 Feb 2000	23 Jan 2001	Metal
2001	24 Jan 2001	11 Feb 2002	Metal
2002	12 Feb 2002	31 Jan 2003	Water
2003	1 Feb 2003	21 Jan 2004	Water
2004	22 Jan 2004	8 Feb 2005	Wood
2005	9 Feb 2005	28 Jan 2006	Wood
2006	29 Jan 2006	17 Feb 2007	Fire
2007	18 Feb 2007	6 Feb 2008	Fire

APPLYING THE KUA FORMULA

Once you know your personal good-health direction, there are several ways you can match your individual chi energies with that of your environment, thus stimulating the healthy sheng chi to your benefit.

Your Kua number offers you your most auspicious direction for safeguarding your physical and mental fitness. It also identifies your luckiest compass location to ensure you do not fall ill easily or succumb to annoying viruses. The luck referred to here is best activated for every member of your family according to each person's most suitable direction and location, as indicated in the Kua number table on pages 26–27.

HOW TO DO IT

The home or apartment layout should be demarcated into the nine sectors according to the Lo Shu grid as shown. To do this accurately, use a good compass (any Western compass will do) and, standing in the center of the home, identify the locations and divide the total floor space of the home into nine equal sectors. This is shown in the diagram.

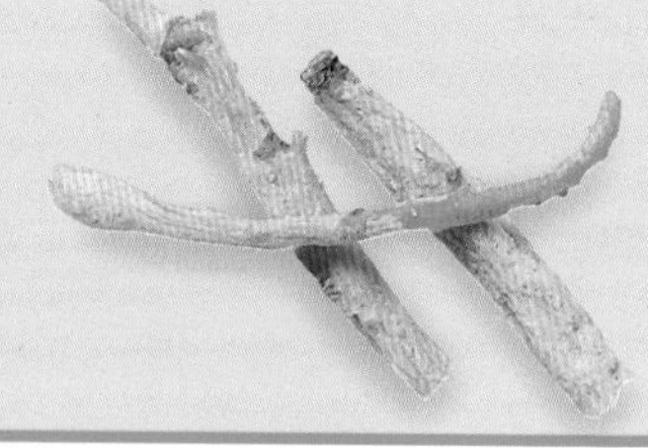

Sleep with your head pointed to the health direction.

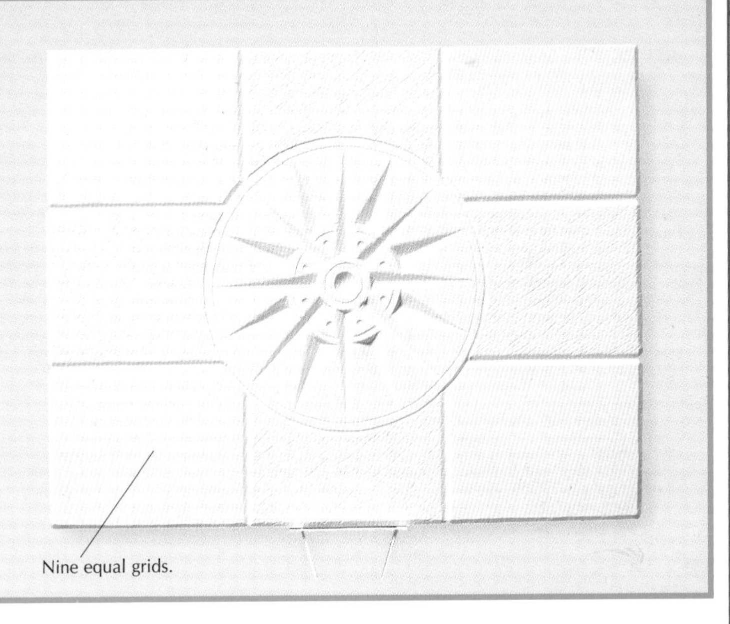

Nine equal grids.

YOUR BEDROOM

Perhaps the best way of capturing good health through the use of this method is to try to match bedrooms to the health locations of the family members and also to try to sleep with the head pointed to the health direction. If your direction is east, for instance, the illustration here shows where your bedroom should be and in what direction your bed should be pointed.

Family members should choose their individual bedrooms according to their health location.

IRREGULAR-SHAPED HOMES

Place a light in your health corner.

Houses and apartments seldom have regular, square, or rectangular shapes, making it difficult to superimpose the nine-sector grid on to the layouts. A serious problem is that of missing corners. According to feng shui, missing corners mean that the home will be lacking in certain luck aspects. What types of luck are missing depend on the corresponding compass directions.

If your health luck corner is missing, hang a wall mirror.

If the shape of your home means that your health corner is missing, then your health luck could be seriously undermined. This may not be a huge problem for those who are still young and in the physical prime of their life, but for people in their fifties and over, when the physical body succumbs more easily to diseases, this feng shui problem should be addressed.

There are ways of getting round this problem and some of these are shown here.

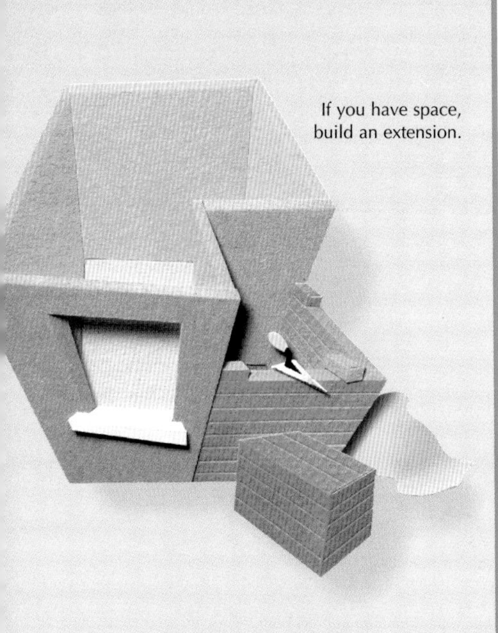
If you have space, build an extension.

If the missing sector represents your health direction, you can partially correct the matter by one of the following methods.

- Install a light.
- Hang a wall mirror.
- Build an extension.

What you do depends on your circumstances and whether you have the available space. However, correcting the problem merely improves the situation; it does not create the good-health luck you want.

THE SLEEPING DIRECTION

An irregular-shaped layout sometimes makes it difficult to locate the bedroom or orient your bed in the way you want. If you cannot get the right location, tapping the health direction alone is often good enough. If you cannot tap either the location or direction, do try to sleep with your head pointed to at least to one of your other auspicious directions (see page 34). Remember that the sleeping direction refers to the direction in which the top of the head points.

The sleeping direction is one of the most vital determinants of good health. Try to sleep with your head pointed to your personal best direction for activating this aspect of your luck. This ensures that each night, even as you sleep, good luck chi is entering your body through your head.

Sleep with your head pointed toward your health direction.

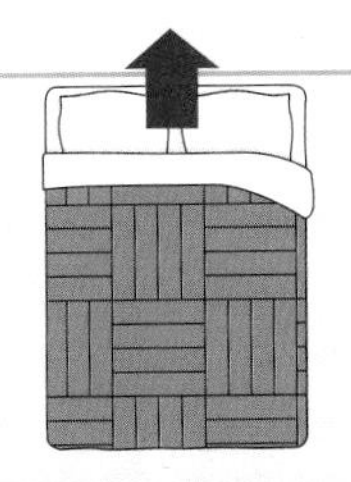

EAST AND WEST GROUP DIRECTIONS

Compass feng shui divides the human race into either east or west group people. Every person is said to have four favorable directions, with each direction representing a different kind of luck. Therefore, in addition to the good-health direction, you will have three other auspicious directions. These depend on whether you are an east or a west group person, which, in turn, depend on your Kua number.

- East group people have Kua numbers one, three, four, and nine.
- East group directions are east, north, south, and southeast.

- West group people have Kua numbers two, five, six, seven, and eight.
- West group directions are west, southwest, northwest, and northeast.

East group directions are inauspicious for west group people and vice versa. Try at all costs to have your main entrance face one of your propitious directions.

EATING WITH YOUR HEALTH IN MIND

Armed with the Kua formula, you can activate personal good-health directions for every member of the family. One way to do this is arranging seating around the family dining table so that every member of the family faces his or her good-health direction. This is easier than it sounds; simply keep a pocket compass in the home.

When you are sitting at your dining table you should make sure that you are facing your auspicious health direction.

However, while using the Pa Kua Lo Shu formula, it is equally essential to observe important rules and guidelines that are part of general form school feng shui. It is important to point out here that no matter how well you may have oriented your beds, chairs, and other furniture in the home, if in so doing you are then inadvertently hit by the pernicious killing breath caused by offensive structures within your immediate vicinity, the killing breath prevails over the good feng shui.

Similarly, there are important feng shui taboos to bear in mind. These are easy to detect and deal with, and are covered in the following pages.

SLEEPING ORIENTATIONS THAT AFFECT HEALTH

THE LOCATION OF YOUR BEDROOM

睡眠

While the Kua formula prescribes the ideal location for your bedroom according to specific compass directions, you must also take account of other factors. Thus, irrespective of where the bedroom is actually located in the home, there are certain guidelines that should be strictly observed to safeguard your health. Much of this has to do with ensuring that you are not attacked by what feng shui Masters refer to as the killing breath; unfriendly energies that bring illness, bad temper, and depression.

Bedrooms located at the end of a long corridor cause ill health, because the flow of energy is too strong, especially if the door into the bedroom is placed at the end of the corridor, as shown on page 37. The situation becomes worse if there is also a door at the other end of the corridor or if the bed inside the bedroom is placed with the feet of the sleeper directly facing the door. Breaking any one of these guidelines attracts health problems for the occupant of the bedroom, and sometimes the energies created can be so strong, the effect may be overwhelming. The way to deal with such a situation is to change the placement of the bed.

The energy in bedrooms located in a part of the building that gets no sunlight at all, or where there are virtually no windows, is said to be too yin. The lack of sunshine and fresh air will make the air stale and the chi becomes stagnant. Bedrooms should be regularly aired and well lit or the consequence will be a build-up of bad chi that manifests itself first in illness, then in other forms of bad luck that follow.

Bedrooms located in a basement, or on a lower floor directly below a toilet, washing machine, or cooker on the upper floor are considered inauspicious. Bad, harmful chi is created on a daily basis and affects the health of the people sleeping below. The worst situation is for a person to sleep beneath a toilet. Avoid this at all costs.

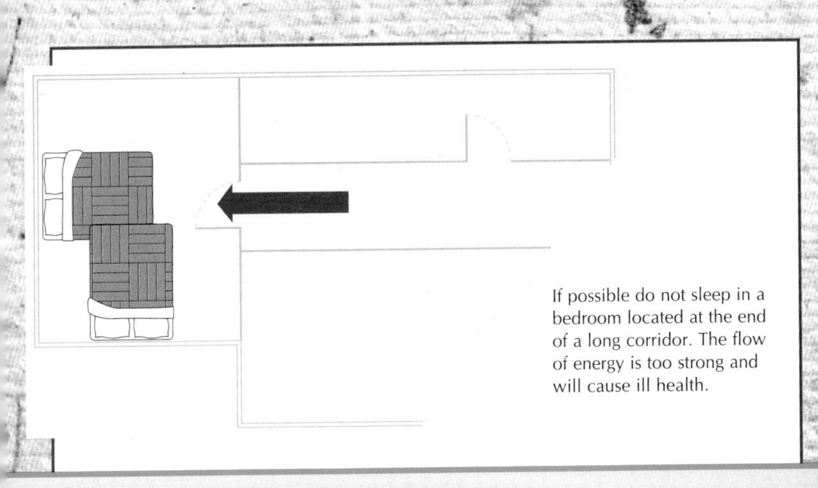

If possible do not sleep in a bedroom located at the end of a long corridor. The flow of energy is too strong and will cause ill health.

POSITIONING YOUR BED

Avoid sleeping beneath a toilet.

Harmful chi will affect a person sleeping beneath a washing machine.

It is considered inauspicious to sleep below a cooker.

THE POSITION AND ORIENTATION OF THE BED

Make sure your bed is located in an auspicious place according to form school feng shui before attempting to tap your best health direction. It is always advisable to start out by first protecting yourself from what feng shui practitioners term hidden poison arrows. Watch out for any offensive features or structures that may inadvertently be sending poison arrows of bad chi toward you as you sleep. These cause headaches, migraines, and other forms of illness. Focus on the placement of the bed inside the room itself.

The arrow in the illustration shows you how to take the direction in the correct way. Note that the head should be pointed in the auspicious direction. If you and your partner have different auspicious directions, sleep in two separate beds. Note that the bed is placed diagonally to the door. This is the best placement from a feng shui perspective.

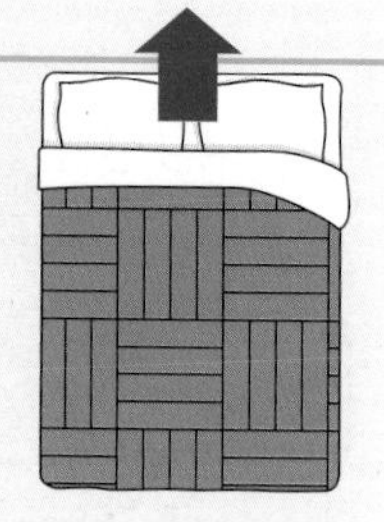

PRACTICAL GUIDELINES

To safeguard the harmony of the home, the position of the bedrooms in the overall layout is also important. Try to select a bedroom that does not have any of the following features and also to observe some of these practical guidelines.

- Try to ensure that the bedroom door does not open directly to a toilet. Nor should the bed be placed against a wall that is shared by a toilet.
- Try to avoid having a bedroom door that opens directly on to a staircase, as this causes unfortunate chi to enter the bedroom, hurting the occupant.
- Try not to have the bedroom door directly face the corner edge of another room. This causes a blockage of chi, resulting in circulatory ailments for the occupant of the room.
- If a room has previously been occupied by someone very ill, it is a good idea to give it a good airing before allocating it to someone else. Install a bright light, paint the room a bright, happy colour and turn on the music. This re-introduces much-needed yang energy.

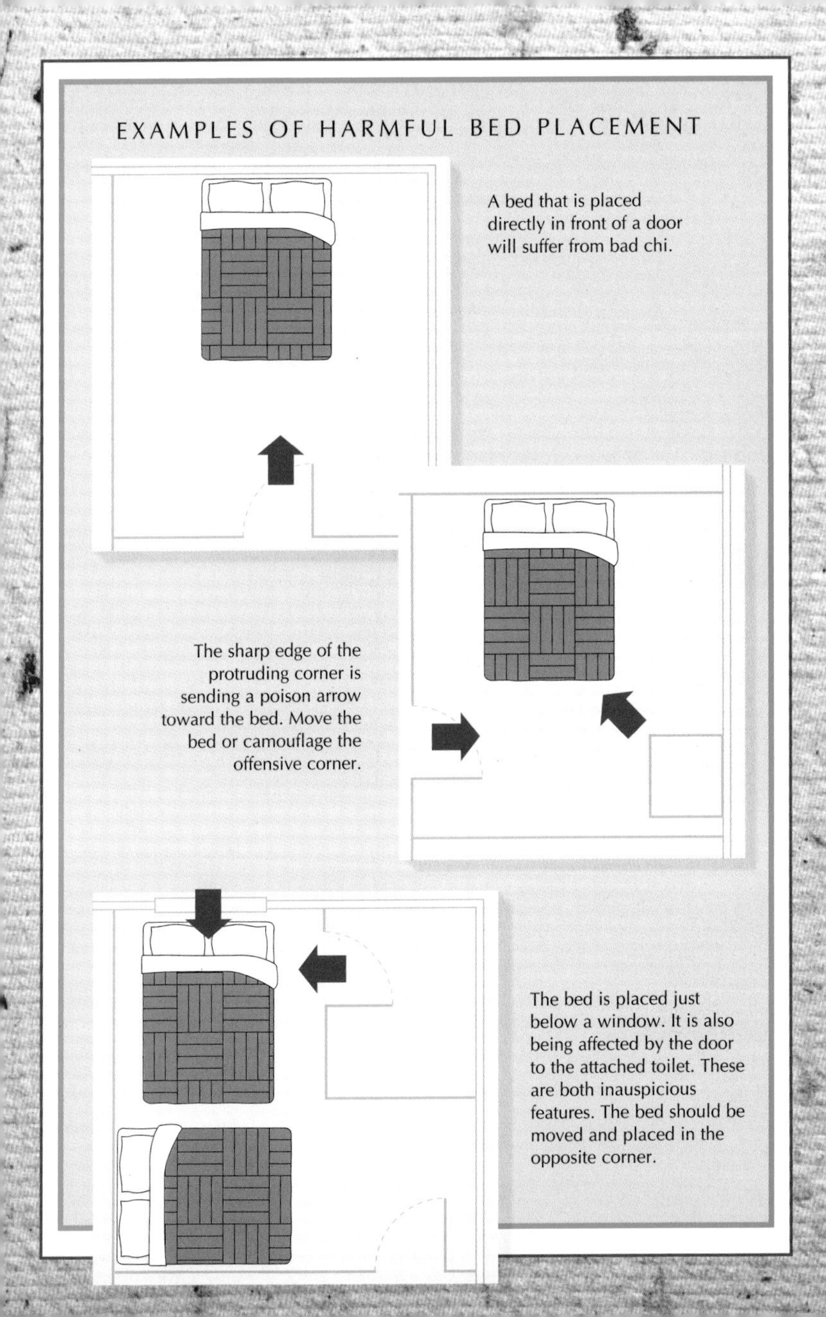
EXAMPLES OF HARMFUL BED PLACEMENT
A bed that is placed directly in front of a door will suffer from bad chi.
The sharp edge of the protruding corner is sending a poison arrow toward the bed. Move the bed or camouflage the offensive corner.
The bed is placed just below a window. It is also being affected by the door to the attached toilet. These are both inauspicious features. The bed should be moved and placed in the opposite corner.

SLEEPING TABOOS

Never sleep with a mirror facing the bed. A television is regarded as the same as a mirror because it too reflects. If you have a television in the bedroom, cover it when it is not in use. A mirror in the bedroom is one of the most harmful of feng shui features. Apart from causing havoc in the relationship between two partners, a mirror facing the bed creates health problems connected with the heart. This is because mirrors are said to represent the water element and while you are asleep, this attacks the internal organ represented by the fire element – the heart. This is why feng shui Masters often advise that mirrors installed on cupboard doors and dressing tables should either be covered or moved somewhere else. Mirrors above the bed are equally harmful.

Never sleep with a water feature behind your bed. It is not a good idea to have a painting of a lake or waterfall above your bed because it has the same effect on the heart as a mirror. Worse than a painting is the presence of actual water, such as a fish tank. While water and fish are excellent features to attract wealth, they are distinctly out of place in the bedroom.

Never sleep under an exposed overhead beam. The severity of the negative chi depends on where the beam crosses the bed. If it is directly above the head, migraines and headaches will be common occurences. If it crosses at chest level, it creates problems associated with the lungs and heart, as well as causing susceptibility to the common cold and other respiratory ailments. If beds are affected by a beam, move the bed out of the way. If this is not possible, try to camouflage the beam by installing a false ceiling. Remember that exposed overhead beams are bad from a feng shui perspective and will always cause

Sheets and the decor of bedrooms should ideally be in more muted yin colors unless the bedroom has been diagnosed as being too yin: if it is badly lit, has no windows, or had been previously occupied by someone who has recently died.

A landscape painting that features water is unsuitable for the bedroom.

A water feature, such as a bowl of water, a vase of flowers, or, worse, a fish tank, is sadly out of place in the bedroom. Having any of these features present is never encouraged.

An overhead beam and a television are both very bad feng shui features in the bedroom. Avoid them if possible

problems, whether you are sitting, sleeping, or working directly beneath them.

Never sleep with the sharp edge of a protruding corner pointed at you. This is a common problem. Many bedrooms have such corners and they are as harmful as free-standing pillars. The sharp edge of a corner is one of the most deadly forms of poison arrow that brings with it shar chi, the killing breath. Anyone who s;eeps in the path of the poison arrows will suffer from constant health problems. The best solution is to block off or camouflage the corner. Using plants is an ideal solution in the living room, but the presence of plants in the bedroom is not such a good idea; it is better to use a piece of furniture to disguise the edge.

THE KITCHEN

THE KITCHEN LOCATION

The kitchen should be located within the home, in relation to the main breadwinner's Kua number. The text on Kua formula feng shui gives the following general guidelines for the auspicious location of the kitchen within the family home.

THE KITCHEN DOOR

Be aware of the way the doors around the kitchen area are located in relation to each other. The kitchen door should not be in a straight line from either the front door or the back door. This is a most inauspicious configuration. Bad luck will slowly accumulate, manifesting itself first in annoying illness, then progressing to more serious misfortunes, especially if two or, worse still, three doors are left open regularly.

GUIDELINES

- Kitchens should be located in the inner half of the home.
- Kitchens should not directly face the main front door. Any good fortune chi that enters the home is immediately destroyed in such a house layout.
- Kitchens should never directly face a bedroom. The energies of such a floor plan clash particularly badly, because a bedroom is yin and a kitchen is yang. Continuous illness of family members will result from such a configuration, due to the imbalance between the yin and yang energy.
- Other guidelines on kitchen location match the do's and don'ts applicable to all the other rooms and doors of the home.

WEST GROUP PEOPLE

Those with Kua numbers two, six, seven, and eight should try to locate their kitchens, especially their ovens, in places within the home that represent the east. Kitchens should be in the east, north, south, or southeast part of the home. This ensures that the kitchen will suppress any of the bad luck areas within the home and residents will enjoy good health and good fortune. If the kitchen lies in any of the west group directions, the good luck of the family breadwinner is seriously undermined, and the whole family suffers.

EAST GROUP PEOPLE

It follows that those with Kua numbers one, three, four, and nine are strongly advised to have their kitchens located in one of the auspicious west group locations. These are west, southwest, northwest, or northeast. The kitchen will then counteract all the family's bad luck locations, thereby ensuring material well-being and good health for all the members of the family. If the kitchen is in any of the auspicious east group locations, good luck will be missing and inevitable loss and ill-health will be the result.

Ideally place the cooker in the south, southwest, or northeast.

Do not locate the sink next to the cooker.

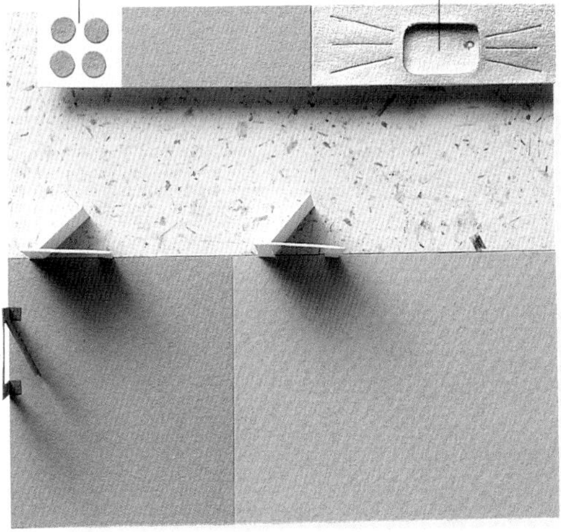

Kitchens should not face the main door.

Locate the kitchen in the most auspicious direction for the family breadwinner.

THE COOKER

While feng shui recommends that the kitchen itself should be located in one of the personally inauspicious locations of your home, based on the Kua compass formula, the ancient texts also advise that the "mouth" of the cooker should face one of your auspicious directions, especially your health direction (see pages 26-27). This means that the source of the energy for cooking your food should come from an auspicious direction.

In the past, it was easy to identify the "mouth" of the stove, since wood or charcoal was always used for cooking, but it is more difficult with modern appliances. Generally the "mouth" is defined by feng shui masters as the exact place where energy (electricity, gas, or oil) enters. To the Chinese, whose staple food is rice, this is an easy guideline to follow, since all that is needed is to orient the rice cooker in a way that meets these feng shui criteria.

FIRE AND WATER CLASH

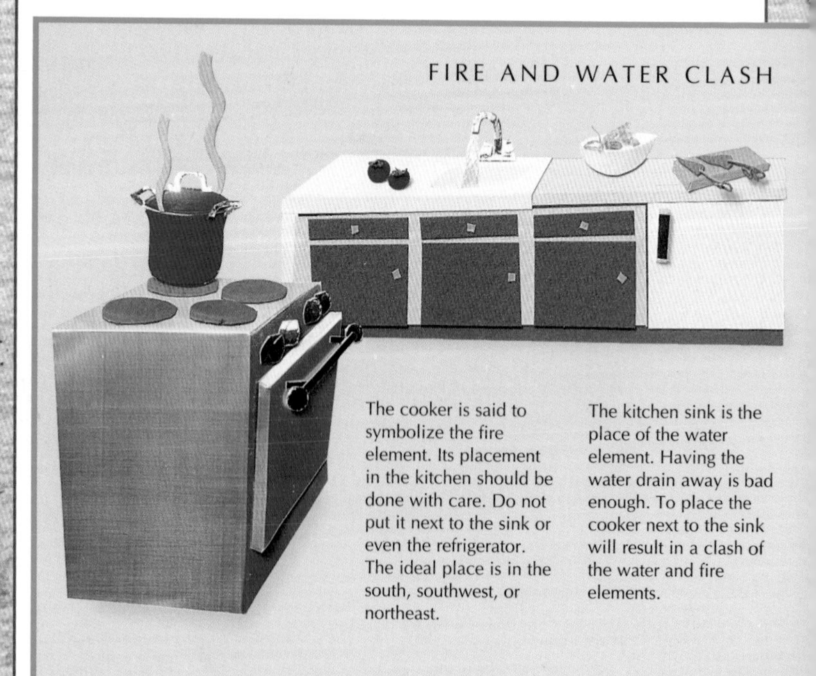

The cooker is said to symbolize the fire element. Its placement in the kitchen should be done with care. Do not put it next to the sink or even the refrigerator. The ideal place is in the south, southwest, or northeast.

The kitchen sink is the place of the water element. Having the water drain away is bad enough. To place the cooker next to the sink will result in a clash of the water and fire elements.

THE COOKER

If you cook most of your meals with a conventional oven, arrange the oven so that the electricity entering the oven is facing your best health direction.

If you use a microwave oven most of the time, then the plug "mouth" where the electricity is connected to the microwave should face your health direction. This ensures excellent health and also brings good fortune.

The oriental rice cooker is perhaps the easiest cooking appliance to manipulate in terms of tapping good feng shui. Just move the cooker until the plug "mouth" (shown here) is directly facing your health direction.

If the occupants of a household belong to different east and west groups, always follow the Kua of the breadwinner. One way to ensure good feng shui for both partners is to have two rice cookers, one facing an east group direction, and another facing a west group direction.

FIRE AT HEAVEN'S GATE

An important kitchen taboo is to guard against placing the cooker in the part of the kitchen that represents the northwest location. Feng shui strenuously warns against setting fire to heaven's gate. This is because the trigram chien, which stands for heaven, the source of all good luck, rules the northwest. Placing a cooker there will result in setting fire to the source of good-luck energy and is not a good idea. Homes with this kind of arrangement are unlucky and residents suffer from ill-health, especially succumbing to heart disease.

COUNTERACTING THE KILLING BREATH

PREVENTION IS BETTER THAN CURE

殺氣

The Chinese view toward health and physical well-being has always been to adopt a preventive approach. It is far better to avoid contracting an illness than to have to cure it. The same attitude is advised in the use of feng shui in the home. It is far better to protect against the foul energies that cause ill health than to allow illness to occur and then to try to cure it. It is better to make certain the feng shui is not bad at the outset than to wait for things to go wrong before applying its guidelines.

In health feng shui, the best approach is to ensure that neither the residents nor any part of the home itself is being attacked by the pernicious killing breath of poison arrows. It is important to make sure that the family is not becoming ill because energies within the home or surrounding the home are either too yin or have become so stale and stagnant they have become harmful.

POISON ARROWS

A pillar, clock tower, cross, windmill, hill, or statue creates bad feng shui if it is located directly in front of your main door. All these structures give out an energy that is too strong and will overwhelm your home, often with sad or tragic consequences. If the main door into your home directly faces any of these structures, the energies are extremely harmful and you should endeavor to block off the view or re-orient the door.

THE KILLING BREATH

In Chinese this is termed shar chi and feng shui always warns that shar chi will bring every kind of misfortune, especially fatal illness and disease. Shar chi is caused by poison arrows; structures that are hostile, threatening, straight, and angular. Whether natural features, such as sharply defined hills or ridges, or manmade constructions, such as massive buildings, offensive structures can sometimes create hostile breath. This will cause a great deal of harm when they are pointed directly at the home, especially at the main door. Many of these structures are external to the home and they are best thought of as arrows. This is because their bad, harmful energy travels in a straight line, taking deadly aim, and "killing" if the invisible arrow of bad energy hits you.

To prevent being harmed by poison arrows, make certain your home, its main door and, in some cases, the windows are not directly facing any of the structures mentioned here.

A main door facing a straight road is the worst possible feng shui; it brings the shar chi straight to your door. Either re-orient your front door or try to block the fatal energies with a clump of trees or a wall. If the level of your house is above the road, however, it is not harmful.

Even if the edge is not facing your door, when your home opens to an imposing building like this, all the good, healthy chi is blocked and you will suffer from bad feng shui. According to feng shui, the sharp edge of a building is especially harmful.

Living next to a prison, hospital, or cemetery can often cause residents to suffer from illness caused by an excess of yin energies.

DEALING WITH ENERGIES THAT ARE TOO YIN

The physical well-being of residents is often affected and they succumb more easily to illness when the energies that surround their home are too yin. The theory of feng shui always requires there to be a harmonious balance of yin and yang energies. When there is too much yin energy, health suffers; often more so than when there is too much yang energy. This is because yin is representative of death, while yang is symbolic of life.

Yin energies are considered to be much too strong and overwhelming when your home is located in the vicinity of a police station, cemetery, hospital, slaughterhouse, or any other place associated with despair, death, and illness. It is worse if your home is situated right next to any of these places. Some feng shui practitioners go so far as to investigate the history of the land where a new home is to be sited or the previous use of buildings that are to be converted into residential apartments. Feng shui contends that the energies of previous occupants linger and when these are sickly or weak, the energies are very yin. Consequently, if your home is located on a site that formerly housed a hospital or a prison, indications will be that the place is too yin, often to a harmful extent..

If you have a choice, it is advisable not to have a home near such places. Otherwise, the way to deal with excessive yin energy is to introduce healthy doses of yang energy.

ROOMS THAT ARE TOO YIN

A room that is excessively yin is one that has previously been occupied by someone very ill, that has no windows, or has not been cleaned for several years so the energies within have been allowed to grow stale and stagnant. If you move into such a room, then even if you sleep with your head pointed in your health direction, you will succumb to the bad energies. In this case, repaint the room or clear out the stagnant energy by giving it a good scrub and installing bright lights. Then play some music in there to liven up the atmosphere.

PLAY MUSIC

Sounds, especially happy ones, are a wonderful antidote to excessive yin energy. Keep the radio or television playing the entire day, even when you are not at home, and especially if you are living by yourself. Sounds activate the living space and clear out stale, stagnant energies.

Keep the area just outside your main door brightly lit at all times. The bright light is symbolic of powerful yang energy and is most effective in ensuring a more auspicious balance of yin and yang. Spotlights are ideal, but porch lights are just as effective. Paint your main front door a bright, happy red. This is a most effective way of countering excessive yin energy and could even bring better luck.

COUNTERACTING STALE AND STAGNANT ENERGY

When the energies around and within a home become stale and stagnant, the health of the residents suffers. This is regarded as one of the most common causes of poor health. People constantly succumb to the common cold, stomach ulcers, and other ailments.

Stale chi is principally created when the air within the home has not been cleared out. During dark winter days, when windows stay closed for long periods, it is easy for the chi inside the home to stagnate. If there is also clutter and dirt, the situation is seriously compounded. This is because winter is also the cold season of yin, when yang energy is in short supply. A preponderance of yin energy at this time of year can therefore lead to illness, lethargy, and even depression.

Keeping the home well heated and well lit creates healthy yang energy. Of course, it also creates much-needed warmth. More importantly, it causes energies to become balanced and fresh. Playing lively music also generates happy chi. This is why it is always a good idea to have a Christmas tree in the house. Decorating the tree with sparkling ornaments and lights will ensure that wonderful healthy chi is created. Beautiful and inspiring choral music will also add happy chi to the living space.

All the symbols and decorations of the Christmas season bring healthy yang energy – candles, lights, bells, red ribbons, colorful ornaments hung on brightly lit trees. It is the same with the seasonal celebrations or festivals of most other cultures.

The use of lights at times of celebration, like the candles lit by these Buddhists in Shanghai, fills the air with healthy chi.

'SPRING' CLEANING

Perhaps it is a subconscious need to clean up the home to clear its energies that has led peoples of all backgrounds and cultures to undertake a thorough cleaning prior to celebrating traditional happy occasions – although not only in the spring. As it is for Jews celebrating Passover, so it is, too, for the Chinese celebrating the lunar New Year and for the Muslims celebrating Eid al-Fitr after a month of fasting during Ramadan, a practice that is believed to cleanse the body and the mind. Almost all traditional happy occasions are times when lights are used lavishly. The people of the Indian subcontinent, for example, celebrate Diwali, also known as the Festival of Lights.

To enjoy healthy feng shui in your living space, it is vital that the home be kept clean and free of clutter. Blocked drains should be cleared. Plumbing represents the arteries of the home, and any blockage can cause serious illness when not attended to. Appliances that have broken down should be repaired. You should get rid of polluted or dirty water in the garden and if the toilet or bathroom become clogged, the problem should be attended to immediately. All of this may seem to be good sound common sense, but it is surprising how often simple repair chores are put off. From a feng shui point of view, this is unhealthy.

Clear any blockages in your plumbing system.

THE TIME DIMENSION

USING FLYING STAR FENG SHUI

時间

Flying star feng shui is a very popular method used in Hong Kong, Malaysia, and Singapore that addresses the time aspects of feng shui. Flying star adds the vital dynamics of changes brought about by the passage of time, while complementing the space dimension of all other feng shui methods. This is a very advanced method and it is not necessary for amateur practitioners to become too involved in its technical details. However, it is useful to have a reference table to enable you to investigate the impact of flying star on your own feng shui, particularly since this method is excellent for warning against the flying stars that bring illness.

WHAT ARE THE FLYING STARS?

These are the numbers one to nine placed around a nine-sector grid, known as the Lo Shu magic square. The numbers around the grid fly, changing with the passage of time. Every month and year and every 20-year period has its own arrangement of numbers around the square. Every number has its own meanings. For the feng shui expert who knows how to interpret the numbers a great deal of information can be gleaned from each arrangement.

SOUTH

4	9	2
3	5	7
8	1	6

THE PERIOD OF SEVEN

We are currently living through the period of seven, which started in 1984 and will not end until the year 2003. This means that during this period, the number seven is deemed to be very lucky. The Lo Shu square for this period is shown here and, through an interpretation of the numbers, it describes the fortunate and less fortunate sectors up to the year 2003.

SOUTH

6	2	4
5	7	9
1	3	8

The original nine-sector Lo Shu square has the number five in the center. The numbers are arranged so that the sum of any three numbers, taken vertically, horizontally, or diagonally, is 15. In flying star feng shui, the numbers move from grid to grid and they are then interpreted according to which one is in which square. Each of the eight grids on the outside of the square represents a corner of the home. For analysis, the center is the ninth grid. South is placed on top, according to tradition, for presentation purposes only. Use a compass to identify the actual corners of your home.

During the period of seven, the sickness stars, two and five, are located in the south and east respectively. This is interpreted to mean that if the main door of your home is located in either of these sectors, residents will be more susceptible to sickness. It also means that those sleeping in bedrooms located in these sectors are more prone to suffering ill-health.

The analysis will be more accurate when investigation is also conducted on the star numerals during the year and month in question. When all of the star numerals two and five occur together in the same sector, illness is definite during that month and year for people whose bedrooms are in that sector. When you become aware of the time when you are more prone to falling ill, do not sleep in the room afflicted by the numerals two or five for that month.

Year	Star numeral 2 is in the	Star numeral 5 is in the
1997	Southeast	West
1998	Center	Northeast
1999	Northwest	South
2000	West	North
2001	Northeast	Southwest
2002	South	East
2003	North	Southeast
2004	Southwest	Center
2005	East	Northwest
2006	Southeast	West

Year	Month 1	Month 2	Month 3	Month 4	Month 5
1997	Southwest	East Northwest	Southeast West	Northeast	South Northwest
1998	Northeast	Northwest South	West North	Northeast Southwest	South East
1999	Northeast Southwest	South East	North Southeast	Southwest	East Northwest
2000	Southwest	East Northwest	Southeast West	Northeast	Northwest South
2001	Northeast	Northwest South	West North	Northeast Southwest	South East

ROOMS TO AVOID DURING SPECIFIC PERIODS

*The yearly reference table (*based on the lunar year)*

The table opposite shows where the star five and star two occur together. The star two combined with star five is very dangerous, and will bring sickness.

THE MONTHLY REFERENCE TABLES

*(*based on the lunar months)*

The table below indicates the dangerous sectors during each of the 12 lunar months over the next five years. These are the sectors where the star numerals two and five are located during that month. In the years 1998 and 2001 there are 13 months, so one of the months has been doubled.

Match where the star numerals two and five fall during the months indicated with those of the annual star numerals and the 20-year period star numerals.

If the twos and fives occur together, that sector will become dangerous and anyone occupying a room in an afflicted sector would do well to leave it for that time. Be particularly careful when the star numerals two and five fall into the east sector. This is because the eastern sector is afflicted with the five in the 20-year period flying star. The danger months and the directions are marked. When there are two dots, it means that both the sectors indicated are dangerous.

Based on the reference table left, rooms in the south are prone to illness in 1999. In 2002 rooms in the south and east should be avoided and in 2005 rooms in the east should be avoided.

Month 6	Month 7	Month 8	Month 9	Month 10	Month 11	Month 12
West North	Northeast Southwest	South East	North Southeast	Southwest	East Northwest	Southeast West
South East	North Southeast	Southwest	East Northwest	Southeast West	Northeast	Northwest South
Southeast West	Northeast	Northwest South	West North	Northeast Southwest	South East	North Southeast
West North	Northeast Southwest	South East	North Southeast	Southwest	East Northwest	Southeast West
North Southeast	Southwest	East Northwest	Southeast West	Northeast	Northwest South	West North

INDEX

FURTHER READING

Kwok, Man-Ho and O'Brien, Joanne, *The Elements of Feng Shui,* ELEMENT BOOKS, SHAFTESBURY, 1991

Lo, Raymond *Feng Shui: The Pillars of Destiny (Understanding Your Fate and Fortune),* TIMES EDITIONS, SINGAPORE, 1995

Skinner, Stephen, *Living Earth Manual of Feng Shui: Chinese Geomancy,* PENGUIN, 1989

Too, Lillian, *The Complete Illustrated Guide to Feng Shui,* ELEMENT BOOKS, SHAFTESBURY, 1996

Too, Lillian *Basic Feng Shui,* KONSEP BOOKS, KUALA LUMPUR, 1997

Too, Lillian *Chinese Astrology for Romance and Relationships* , KONSEP BOOKS, KUALA LUMPUR, 1996

Too, Lillian *Chinese Numerology in Feng Shui,* KONSEP BOOKS, KUALA LUMPUR, 1994

Too, Lillian *Dragon Magic,* KONSEP BOOKS, KUALA LUMPUR, 1996

Too, Lillian *Feng Shui,* KONSEP BOOKS, KUALA LUMPUR, 1993

Too, Lillian *Practical Applications for Feng Shui,* KONSEP BOOKS, KUALA LUMPUR, 1994

Too, Lillian *Water Feng Shui for Wealth,* KONSEP BOOKS, KUALA LUMPUR, 1995

Walters, Derek *Feng Shui Handbook: A Practical Guide to Chinese Geomancy and Environmental Harmony,* AQUARIAN PRESS, 1991

USEFUL ADDRESSES

Feng Shui Design Studio
PO Box 705, Glebe, Sydney, NSW 2037, Australia, Tel: 61 2 315 8258

Feng Shui Society of Australia
PO Box 1565, Rozelle, Sydney NSW 2039, Australia

The Geomancer
The Feng Shui Store
PO Box 250, Woking, Surrey GU21 1YJ
Tel: 44 1483 839898
Fax: 44 1483 488998

Feng Shui Association
31 Woburn Place, Brighton BN1 9GA,
Tel/Fax: 44 1273 693844

Feng Shui Network International
PO Box 2133, London W1A 1RL,
Tel: 44 171 935 8935,
Fax: 44 171 935 9295

The School of Feng Shui
34 Banbury Road, Ettington, Stratford-upon-Avon, Warwickshire CV37 7SU. Tel/Fax: 44 1789 740116

The Feng Shui Institute of America
PO Box 488, Wabasso, FL 32970,
Tel: 1 407 589 9900 Fax: 1 407 589 1611

Feng Shui Warehouse
PO Box 3005, San Diego, CA 92163,
Tel: 1 800 399 1599 Fax: 1 800 997 9831

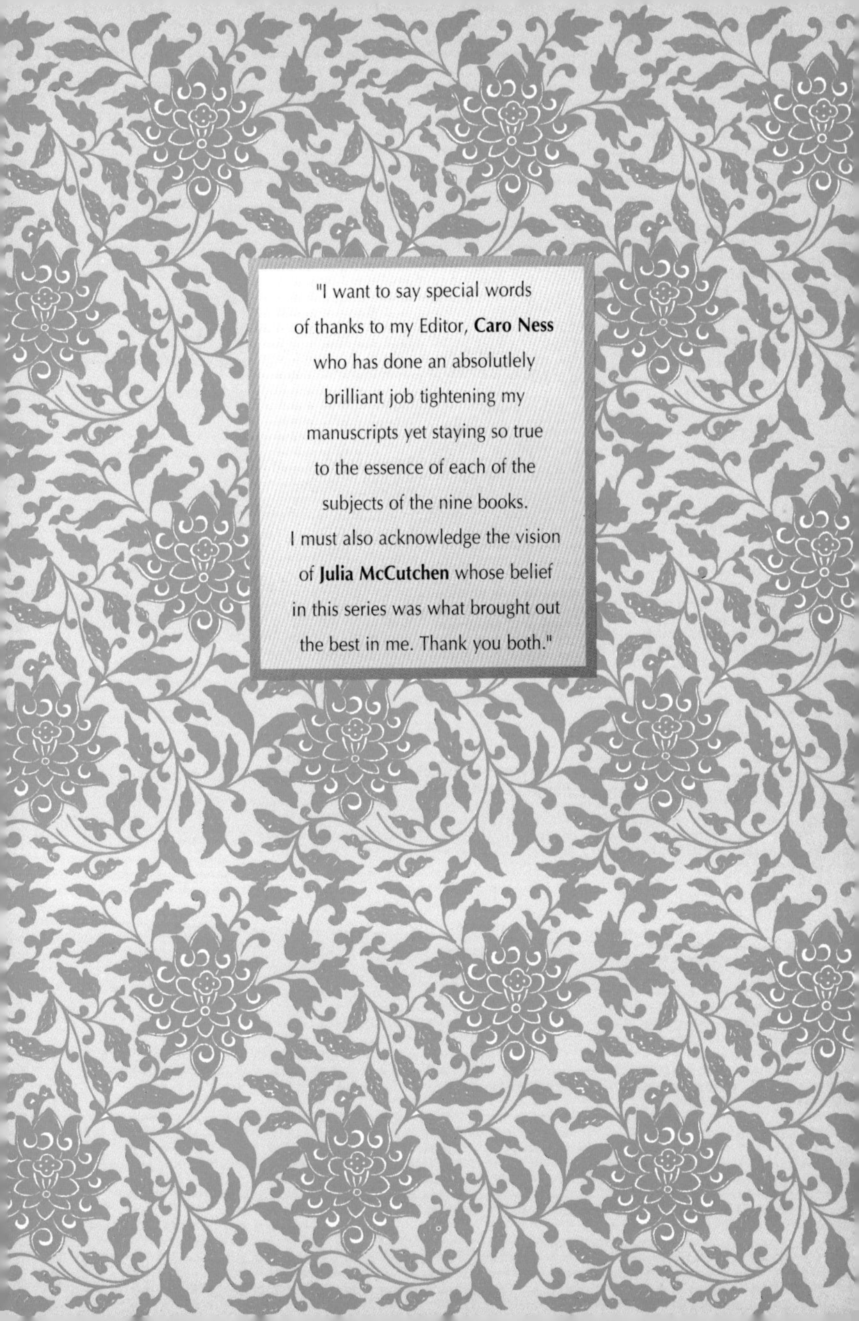
"I want to say special words
of thanks to my Editor, **Caro Ness**
who has done an absolutlely
brilliant job tightening my
manuscripts yet staying so true
to the essence of each of the
subjects of the nine books.
I must also acknowledge the vision
of **Julia McCutchen** whose belief
in this series was what brought out
the best in me. Thank you both."

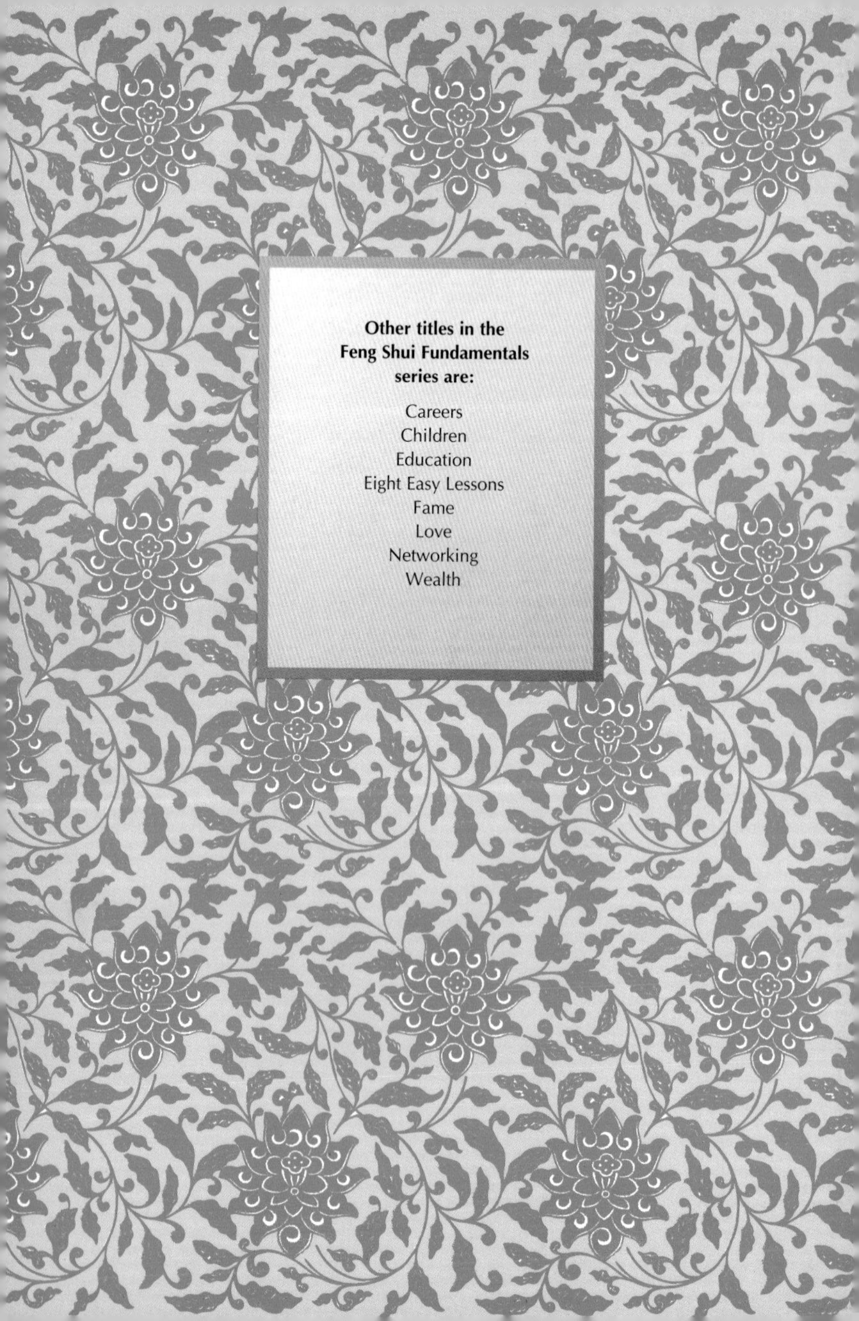

Other titles in the Feng Shui Fundamentals series are:

Careers
Children
Education
Eight Easy Lessons
Fame
Love
Networking
Wealth